Proofread
Your Essay

Sara Miller McCune founded SAGE Publishing in 1965 to support the dissemination of usable knowledge and educate a global community. SAGE publishes more than 1000 journals and over 800 new books each year, spanning a wide range of subject areas. Our growing selection of library products includes archives, data, case studies and video. SAGE remains majority owned by our founder and after her lifetime will become owned by a charitable trust that secures the company's continued independence.

Los Angeles | London | New Delhi | Singapore | Washington DC | Melbourne

SUPER
QUICK
SKILLS

Proofread Your Essay

Louise Connolly

Los Angeles | London | New Delhi
Singapore | Washington DC | Melbourne

Los Angeles | London | New Delhi
Singapore | Washington DC | Melbourne

SAGE Publications Ltd
1 Oliver's Yard
55 City Road
London EC1Y 1SP

SAGE Publications Inc.
2455 Teller Road
Thousand Oaks, California 91320

SAGE Publications India Pvt Ltd
B 1/I 1 Mohan Cooperative Industrial Area
Mathura Road
New Delhi 110 044

SAGE Publications Asia-Pacific Pte Ltd
3 Church Street
#10-04 Samsung Hub
Singapore 049483

Editor: Jai Seaman
Editorial assistant: Hannah Cavender-Deere
Production editor: Rachel Burrows
Marketing manager: Catherine Slinn
Cover design: Shaun Mercier
Typeset by: C&M Digitals (P) Ltd, Chennai, India

Library of Congress Control Number: 2021949317

British Library Cataloguing in Publication data

A catalogue record for this book is available from
the British Library

ISBN 978-1-5297-9262-1

Contents

Everything in
this book!

Section 1   Why do I need to proofread my essay?

In this section, you will find out why it is important to proofread your writing, what it entails, as well as reflecting on your current confidence levels when checking your writing.

Section 2   What is the best time and place to proofread my writing?

The environment and time you choose to complete your proofreading is important and can make a big difference! Find out when and where is best in this section.

Section 3   How can I proofread for clarity in my writing?

When you read your own writing, it is easy to assume everyone else will understand what you are trying to say. This isn't always the case! Find out how to be clearer in this section.

Section 4 Should I avoid certain words or phrases when writing essays?

Yes! Some words can be imprecise, judgemental or vague. This section will help you to avoid using such words which could affect the meaning and tone of your writing.

Section 5 How can I check my spelling, punctuation and grammar?

Are you unsure where to start when checking for errors? This section includes lots of top tips that will help make sure you are communicating effectively, including some common errors to look out for.

Section 6 How can I ensure my writing content is appropriate?

When writing an essay you are usually provided with guidance about the suggested content of your assignment. Find out how to use this guidance effectively to ensure you complete what has been asked.

Section 7 How can I add criticality into my essay writing?

Students frequently get feedback like 'Try to add more criticality' or 'You need to include more critical analysis' but what does this mean? This chapter will help you find out.

Section 8 What should I look out for when proofreading for formatting issues?

A lack of attention to formatting can detract from the overall impression. This section will help you ensure your writing is formatted consistently and accurately.

Section 9 Where can I get help or support?

There will be extra support within your university to help with your writing. It's important to find out what support is available and take advantage of it.

Why do I need to proofread my essay?

10 second
summary

Proofreading your writing isn't just reading. It is a much more detailed examination to check for errors and consistency.

60 second
summary

Not proofreading your work carefully is risky!

Proofreading your writing is usually the last stage in the writing process and is essential for any text that will be submitted or read by an intended audience. In a university setting, the audience is likely to be the lecturer or tutor who is marking your assignment.

If you submit work at university that hasn't been thoroughly checked, you run the risk of receiving lower marks because errors in content, style, clarity, grammar and punctuation can reduce the overall impact and cause confusion for the reader.

Proofreading your writing in an effective way can improve the quality and clarity of your writing.

What does proofreading your writing involve?

The review of a final draft of writing usually involves checking content, style and clarity as well as other aspects such as consistency in grammar, punctuation, spelling and formatting.

Proofreading isn't just reading. When you read normally, you tend to skim over individual words and scan for meaning. Proofreading involves a much more detailed examination to check for errors and consistency.

'An effective proofread isn't just reading your writing, it is reading in a detailed and purposeful way.'

Why is it often overlooked?

Proofreading is part of the writing process that can sometimes be forgotten, and this means that errors and inconsistencies are left that could cause confusion. This could even have an impact on your academic writing progress and outcomes.

Students at university often feel they have finished when they have met the word count or included the required content. This is not the case as writing checks are a really important part of the writing and fine-tuning process.

Students also sometimes fail to manage their time appropriately and therefore don't leave enough time before needing to hand in their assignment to thoroughly proofread their writing. This means the proofreading is either not completed or it is very rushed and not purposeful.

How many times do I have to check?

It is easy to think that one check is enough. One check is not enough. To complete a thorough proofread of your writing, you need to complete a number of checks. It also helps to have a break in between proof-reads to make sure you feel refreshed and in the right frame of mind to check carefully.

A student told us

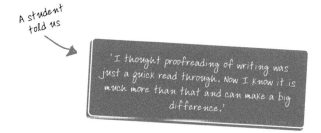

'I thought proofreading of writing was just a quick read through. Now I know it is much more than that and can make a big difference.'

Terminology

There is terminology that you might come across during your time at university that refers to the proofreading process. Some examples are:

Checking	Refining	Reworking
Fine-tuning	Going over	Polishing
Editing	Correcting	Looking through
Analysing	Improving	

You will frequently come across this terminology during your studies because lecturers who mark your work will use them often!

Common problems students report

- 'I never seem to have enough time to proofread my writing! I am always in a rush to just hand it in!'

- 'Because I have written it I find it hard to see errors when reading my own work.'

- 'I don't really know what to look for when I am proofreading my writing.'

- 'In my feedback I always get told to proofread more carefully and I try to, but it doesn't seem to make a difference!'

- 'I know I have poor grammar, but I am embarrassed to ask for help.'

Don't worry! This book will help resolve all these issues!

Use this scale to rate your confidence in your current proofreading skills.

On a scale of 0–5, where 0 = no confidence and 5 = high confidence.

Statement	Confidence level
I understand what proofreading is within my academic studies	
I set aside time to proofread my writing	
I am happy that my writing checks are detailed and helpful	
I always leave enough time to proofread my writing before the assignment has to be handed in	
I know where to get more support with my writing	
I usually carry out more than one check on my academic writing	
Total score	/30

If your score is low, don't worry! This book is here to help you. If your score is high, well done! Keep reading to pick up some more ideas and tips to help you.

What is the best time and place to proofread my writing?

10 second
summary

Careful planning of when and where you will complete your writing checks is essential to support effective checking. This needs to be when you will have fewer distractions around you, enabling you to fully concentrate.

60 second
summary

There is a time and place for everything

Proofreading your writing with lots of noise and people around is not going to be a supportive environment for you to complete a purposeful and detailed check. Consideration needs to be made to ensure that the time and location is going to provide a quiet and relaxed environment, enabling you to have full concentration on the task in hand.

Where you choose to make your checks might be the same place as where you wrote the main content of your essay, and this is fine.

Timing is key

When completing any form of writing, it is important to set time aside to proofread what you have written, and to ensure that this is in advance of your deadline. You could work back from the hand-in date and plan a specific day when you are going to finish your checks to ensure they will be completed in plenty of time, avoiding the need to rush. Make sure you put this date in your diary and consider setting a reminder on your phone too, to make sure you don't forget.

It would be worth having a break between finishing writing your work and proofreading it. This means that you will have a fresh approach and therefore be more likely to spot errors.

On the day of checking, it is best to find a specific time of day when you can avoid distractions or choose to proofread when you know that no one else will be around. Remember that you shouldn't just be completing one check. This means you will need to plan time for several checks with breaks in between.

You will know roughly how long you can concentrate for so make sure you set a time limit after which you will take a break.

A student told us

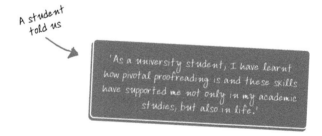

'As a university student, I have learnt how pivotal proofreading is and these skills have supported me not only in my academic studies, but also in life.'

Environment

You need to ensure that there isn't anything in your chosen location that might distract you. This might mean putting your phone elsewhere, or turning your television off, or completing the checks in a room with fewer distractions.

You might find you can concentrate better in a location other than home, such as the university library, so set time aside to go to a different place if necessary.

Should I print my work to check it?

Proofreading a printed version is often found to be easier than onscreen, so consider printing your work to proofread it. This way you can make any changes in pen and then later carry those changes over on the electronic version. Make sure you leave enough time to do this!

'Take your proofreading seriously! Don't see it as just something you are expected to do and therefore go through the motions of doing it without paying close attention.'

Proofreading dos and don'ts

Do	Don't
Plan time to proofread your work.	Leave your proofreading until the last minute.
Identify a specific place to carry out your proofreading.	Complete your proofreading in a noisy and busy environment.
Print out your work to proofread it if possible.	Spend ages staring at the computer screen.
Check your work multiple times.	Only check your work once.
Have breaks in between proofreading.	Attempt to complete your proof-reading when you are tired, or try to complete multiple checks in a short period of time.
Remove distractions such as a mobile phone, TV, etc.	Have lots of distractions around you.
Get in the habit of always proof-reading your writing.	Think you have to proofread your writing only occasionally.

ACTIVITY How effective is my proofreading?

Look at your most recent assignment or writing and answer the following questions:

1 Did you proofread/check this assignment or writing?   Yes/No

2 When and where did you carry out your writing checks?

....

....

....

....

....

....

3 What were the main things you looked for?

....

....

....

....

....

....

4   Do you think your proofreading improved your writing?

....

....

....

....

....

....

....

....

....

Based on your answers, do you think you could have proofread more effectively? How?

....

....

....

....

....

....

....

....

CHECK POINT When and where is my best time and place?

1 My identified location for proofreading my essay is …

....

....

....

....

....

....

....

2 The date I am aiming to proofread my essay is …

....

....

....

....

....

....

....

3 The distracting items I will remove from around me are …

....

....

....

....

....

....

....

....

4 The time of day I think will be best to complete my proofreading is …

....

....

....

....

....

....

....

....

How can I proofread for clarity in my writing?

10 second summary

The most successful writing at university is succinct and communicates key points to the reader very clearly. Proofreading for clarity is an essential skill to develop at university.

60 second summary

Let's make things perfectly clear

Writing with clarity means that you are putting your point across in a clear and succinct way. You should keep to the point, choose your words carefully and write concisely. When you are proofreading for clarity, focus on particular words and phrases to ensure that your meaning has been communicated clearly.

Why do I need to write clearly and concisely?

Whoever is reading your writing needs to have an effortless understanding. If your writing is not clear or easy to follow, it means that the reader might not fully understand the points you are making and will probably lose interest.

In an essay, you will usually be marked on your ability to demonstrate your understanding of a certain topic, and if you are unable to do this clearly it will raise questions about your understanding and could result in lower marks.

Does this mean I need to use long and complicated words?

Sometimes it is easy to fall into the trap of thinking that you need to use words that sound very complicated and 'academic', but this can detract from your writing as you might not fully understand the meaning of the word and therefore use it in the wrong way. It can also result in the focus being drawn away from the key point you are trying to make.

Long and fancy words are not necessarily better than shorter words and you should focus on varying your word choices and ensuring that you are being clear. If you do choose to use an unfamiliar word, make sure you check the meaning in a dictionary before including it in your own writing.

Words that do not add any meaning or clarity are sometimes referred to as 'dead wood'. Instead, you should proofread and look for a clear meaning in your word choices.

For example, in the sentence below there are many words that are unnecessary, and it makes the overall meaning unclear:

> In the event that they commenced to ascertain and decipher the meaning of the undeniably long, complicated and extenuated sentence.

This could be changed to:

> They attempted to ascertain the meaning of the sentence.

During your checks, you may find that you need to add detail to your writing to make it clearer, but you can do this without repeating yourself or adding unnecessary words. For example:

> This section has got four chapters and undeniably endeavours to explain in sufficient detail …

could be changed to:

> This section has four chapters and explains …

'Fancy words don't mean better writing.'

A student told us

'I used to think that I needed to add lots of long words to my essay to sound clever. However, I found I was focusing too much on this and forgetting about the actual content of my writing. Now I am careful that I am not just using long words for the sake of it.'

Don't state the obvious!

Another example of using unnecessary words or phrases is stating things that are obvious or not required. For example:

The conclusion chapter includes the conclusions.

The next point I want to make …

Using unnecessary words could imply to the marker that you have struggled to reach the required word count. This might suggest that there hasn't been a sufficiently detailed discussion within the essay.

Avoid repetition

It is important to ensure you don't repeat the same words frequently as your reader may become bored and lose interest. When proofreading, check for repetition of words. You may find that reading out loud helps with this. You can also use computer applications to help you do this.

You should avoid using the same word twice in a sentence. This can make the content sound repetitive and awkward. It might also make the reader feel they are being told the same thing twice. It is a good idea to find synonyms of the word you have repeated to add variety to your sentences.

I am struggling with the word count!

Another part of the essay proofreading process is checking that the essay has the required number of words and making adjustments if necessary. You might find that you often go over the word limit and therefore need to reduce the number of words used. You can do this by revising the sentence structure and removing unnecessary words. Below are some examples of how to do this:

Word	Reduced to
Adequate amount of	Enough
The majority of	Most
Along the lines of	Like
Identify the location of	Find
Come to the conclusion	Conclude
Despite the fact that	Although
A number of	Several
It is possible that	Perhaps
On the other hand	However

Ideas to reduce the word count …

- Focus on key areas and arguments and be concise.

- Prioritize key points and include more detail for those you think are most significant. Try reducing the detail in less important points or combining a number of key messages into one point.

- Consider removing some adverbs, particularly ones that have '-ly' endings (significantly, relatively, broadly, intensely) as these tend to be 'filler' words that could be left out.

- Check you are sticking to the original question or essay title and remove unnecessary sentences or paragraphs (see Section 6 for more help with this).

Ideas to increase the word count …

- Use additional direct quotes or paraphrase the literature to support key points.

- Add examples to your key points.

- Check you have fully explored the essay question or topic. Word limits are set in terms of expected detail and content, so if you are significantly below the word count it could imply that you have misunderstood or not fully explored the topic.

- Explore more alternative viewpoints – this will mean reading more around the topic.

- Widen your reading to ensure you are referring to multiple sources.

- Seek help from your tutor or lecturer if necessary.

Check some of your own writing for clarity by answering the following questions:

1 Are there any sentences where my choice of words has reduced clarity, or where I have used words in the wrong context? If so, choose one of these sentences and rewrite it more succinctly.

....

....

....

....

....

....

2 Have I added unnecessary words? If so, rewrite the sentence using fewer words so it is more succinct.

....

....

....

....

....

....

3   Have I repeated the same words frequently in my writing? If so, look up synonyms to find alternatives. Write them below.

....

....

....

....

....

....

....

4   Have I used complicated words or terminology associated with the topic which I haven't fully defined for the reader? Choose one of these words and write a definition below, then check in a dictionary.

....

....

....

....

....

....

....

Congratulations

You now know why it is so important to proofread your writing and have thought about your proof-reading habits. You have greater awareness about when and where to complete your writing checks, how to check for clarity and what to look for.

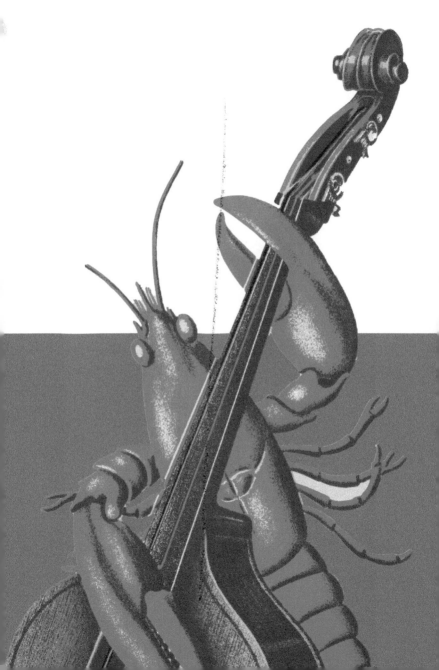

Should I avoid certain words or phrases when writing essays?

10 second summary

The words and phrases you use are important in making sure your assignment is clear and easy to read. Your writing needs to be appropriate for the audience and the word choice plays a big part in this.

60 second summary

What not to say!

When proofreading, you need to make sure your writing makes sense to you but that it also makes sense to the reader. It is important to make sure your writing isn't too informal, that it is concise and the meaning is correctly communicated. To achieve higher standards in academic writing some words or phrases should be avoided.

Thinking carefully about your word choice also helps the flow of your writing and makes it more specific. Knowing what are and are not appropriate ways to communicate is essential.

What kinds of words should I avoid?

There are certain types of colloquial language that should be avoided in academic writing:

- **Slang words or phrases** such as 'kids' and 'stuff' are too vague and imprecise.

- **Clichéd phrases** such as 'As luck would have it' or 'Good things come to those who wait' are commonly used in speech but are best avoided in academic writing.

- **Judgemental words** such as 'nice' or 'horrible' should be avoided. This doesn't mean that you can't express your opinion in your writing, but you should make it clear that it is your own opinion and try to use less judgemental words.

- **Words or phrases that imply sarcasm or humour** should also be avoided in academic writing. Some assignments might be less formal (for example, if you were writing a narration for a presentation) so you should seek guidance from your institution in terms of appropriate use of less formal language.

- **Contractions** such as 'won't', 'wasn't', 'it's' should not be used in academic writing – there is a danger they could weaken a statement or be too informal. These should be changed to 'will not', 'was not', 'it is'. The audience you are writing for makes a difference. You will see that I have used contractions in this book because I am writing more informally than you will be in your academic writing.

- **Vague words** or phrases such as 'big', 'small', 'about', 'kind of' should also be avoided. Your writing needs to be specific and using vague words may imply a lack of understanding.

- **Gendered language** such as 'man', 'women', 'him', or 'she' can be replaced with gender-neutral language like 'they' or 'one'. Alternatively you can rephrase the sentence to remove the need for gender-specific language. This is especially important if you're unsure of the gender of the person or group you are writing about. When you need to use pronouns it's important to check that you're using them correctly. Where gender or sex has been mentioned take the time to ensure that it is necessary or appropriate to do so. Finally, take care to avoid all stereotyping (e.g. occupational stereotypes).

- **Insensitive language** must be avoided. This could include describing someone by unnecessarily drawing attention to their age, race or religion. Care must be taken to ensure that you don't use words that could be insulting or unnecessary. For example, writing 'the Asian doctor' when there is no reason to comment on their ethnicity is bad practice.

- **Biased language** is often the result of the writer making a sweeping generalization without providing any evidence. For example, 'Boys are generally more disruptive than girls'. Sentences like this in your essay will leave the marker thinking 'Says who?' and will reduce the objectivity of your writing. Another example is 'The survey was completed by people from the older generation.' This leaves the reader wondering what constitutes the 'older generation'. It is better to be less descriptive and more specific: 'The survey respondents were between the ages of 65 and 80 years old.'

- **Informal sentence starters** such as 'And', 'Also' or 'So' can sound too informal for an academic essay and can become repetitive if used frequently. Instead, use more formal alternatives such as 'Additionally', 'Furthermore', 'It can be seen that', 'More importantly'.

- **Rhetorical questions** such as 'Should this be seen as a disadvantage?' should be avoided in academic writing – it is assumed that the reader knows the answer but this might not be the case. It is better to use clear and direct language with statements rather than questions. Your writing should be giving the answers, not looking for them!

How to make appropriate word choices in your writing

Look at the following words in red and rewrite the sentences using alternative words or phrases better suited to academic writing.

1 The people were concerned about their stuff.

....

....

....

....

2 The recommendations suggested many things.

....

....

....

....

3 There were found to be many bad research projects.

....

....

....

....

4   The research project had a very big following.

....

....

....

....

5   The research he completed was reliable because ...

....

....

....

....

6   The literature had an awesome and interesting thread.

....

....

....

....

7   The individual was kind of interesting.

....

....

....

....

8 The results were absolutely amazing!

....

....

....

....

A student told us

'I find the best way to make sure my writing reads and flows well is to print out my assignment and read it aloud. I also sometimes use a read-aloud feature on my computer to help me hear the mistakes.'

Become sophisticated!

Using too many simple or informal words in academic writing can make your writing sound unsophisticated. Your writing needs to reflect that you know your subject! Here are some examples of words to avoid and suggested alternatives:

Words to avoid	Suggested alternative
Get 'The research gets recommended.'	Receives 'The research receives recommendation.'
Bad 'There was a bad result.'	Poor, negative 'The results were negative.'
Gives 'This section gives an overview …'	Provides, presents, offers 'This chapter presents an overview …'
Show 'The results show that …'	Demonstrates, indicates, suggests 'The results demonstrate that …'
Kind of 'The results were kind of significant.'	Somewhat, significant to a degree 'The results were significant to a degree.'
Good, great 'A great example …'	Prime, useful 'A prime example …'
Big 'It was a big sample.'	Large, sizeable 'It was a sizeable sample.'

'Repetitive writing makes dull reading. Know what you want to say and make sure others know too!'

Misused words

Sometimes it is easy to use the wrong word, which can affect the meaning of a sentence. This is something you should look out for when proofreading your writing and also highlights the importance of reading your writing very carefully. Some common examples of these are shown below:

- Averse, adverse
    - Averse – having a feeling of dislike
    - Adverse – harmful or unfavourable
- Except, accept
    - Except – leaving out or excluding
    - Accept – to receive something willingly
- Assent, ascent
    - Assent – to agree or approve
    - Ascent – rising upwards
- Precede, proceed
    - Precede – to come or go before
    - Proceed – to go forward or begin a course of action
- Principal, principle
    - Principal – first in order of importance or senior person
    - Principle – a truth or rule of governing behaviour

Have I avoided?

- ☐ Slang words or phrases
- ☐ Clichéd words or phrases
- ☐ Judgemental words
- ☐ Inappropriate humour or sarcasm
- ☐ Contractions
- ☐ Vague words
- ☐ Gendered language
- ☐ Insensitive language
- ☐ Biased language
- ☐ Informal sentence starters
- ☐ Rhetorical questions

How can I check my spelling, punctuation and grammar?

10 second
summary

You might have lots of interesting content in your writing, but if it is poorly spelt, punctuated or constructed this will detract from the overall quality of your writing.

60 second summary

You're going to need to check your essay carefully!

Correct spelling, punctuation and grammar are important to enable you to communicate key messages clearly in your essay. Errors in these areas can change the meaning of your sentences and make it difficult for the reader to figure out what you are trying to say.

If you eliminate these errors in your writing you will find that you create a much better impression on the reader.

As a university student, you are the essay writer. Grammar and punctuation are your tools, and they shouldn't be taken for granted. You will need to spend time reviewing or developing your knowledge in these areas.

What are the top tips for proofreading for spelling, punctuation and grammar?

- Read your assignment out loud or use a read-aloud feature on your computer, being careful to follow your punctuation to identify incorrect punctuation or sentence structure.

- Consider using a ruler to look at one line at a time. This will guide your eyes more easily and encourage you to focus.

- Try to focus on reading one word at a time to check for any errors. This will mean you will probably read more slowly than usual.

- Once you have proofread your own work, it is always useful to ask someone else to proofread it as well. We sometimes can't notice our own mistakes.

A student told us

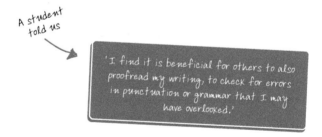

'I find it is beneficial for others to also proofread my writing, to check for errors in punctuation or grammar that I may have overlooked.'

- If you or one of your tutors has identified a particular area of weakness in spelling, punctuation or grammar, you should increase your knowledge in this area and focus on this more when proofreading. You might also consider proofreading for one frequent error category at a time. For example, only looking at commas if this is an area of weakness.

- You should read through your writing several times. You could choose to focus on punctuation or spelling or grammar each time.

- Ask for help. If you come across something you are not sure about when proofreading, you should seek help from your educational institution.

What are common grammatical and punctuation errors to look out for?

There are some common errors in punctuation and grammar you should pay particular attention to when proofreading.

Apostrophes

There are different types of apostrophes, and it is important to use the correct one in your writing.

Correct use of apostrophes

1   To indicate a missing letter or letters, e.g. 'I can't' meaning 'I cannot', 'don't' meaning 'do not'. (Remember not to use contractions in academic writing.)

2   To indicate possession.
    o   'The girl's essay' (singular – if there is one owner, the apostrophe goes *before* the s).

    o   'In the final assessment, the students' assignments scored very highly' (plural possession – if there is more than one owner, the apostrophe goes *after* the s).

An apostrophe is not used to write plural forms, e.g. 'bananas for sale' is correct, 'banana's for sale' is incorrect; 'I've got lots of books' (correct), 'I've got lots of book's' (incorrect).

Paragraphs

Paragraphs are important in organizing your ideas and guiding the reader, like stepping stones. Common errors are to either have too many paragraphs or too few. A paragraph might also be too long or too short. It is important that you understand the features and purpose of a paragraph in your writing.

An easy way to learn when a new paragraph is needed is to follow the acronym TiPToP

- Ti – stands for time. Start a new paragraph for a different time period.

- P – stands for place. Start a new paragraph for each new place.

- To – stands for topic. Start a new paragraph when writing about a different topic or theme.

- P – stands for person. Start a new paragraph when writing about a new person.

Commas

Commas can perform many different functions, which is exactly why using them can be confusing. Using commas is important in your writing as they help with the general flow and understanding. A common error is a comma splice. This is when two independent clauses are joined by a comma which should instead be linked by a colon, semi-colon or conjunction.

For example, 'I finished my essay, I did not hand it in' should instead be one of the following:

- 'I finished my essay, but I did not hand it in.'

- 'I finished my essay; I did not hand it in.'

- 'I completed my essay, although I have not handed it in.'

Homophones

Homophones are words that can sound the same but have a different spellings and meanings, such as there/their/they're, where/wear, who's/whose, to/two/too. It is important to check that you have used the correct word choice in the context or sentence.

Colons and semicolons

Colons and semicolons help organize your ideas and signpost them more clearly.

- A colon usually precedes a list or explanation or introduces a quoted sentence.

- A semicolon is used to link two independent, closely related clauses.

'Clarity goes beyond just word choice. You can't just select words and expect the reader to put them together. That is your job!'

Reflect on your feedback

You should take careful note of feedback you have previously received and use this to identify the punctuation or grammatical errors that you need to focus on when proofreading.

What software support is available?

There are now lots of apps available that can provide support for spelling, grammar and punctuation. These might be particularly useful if you are aware that spelling, grammar or punctuation are areas of weakness for you.

Applications like Microsoft Word have features that can be activated in order to identify errors. However, these are not foolproof and therefore shouldn't be completely relied upon. You should still carefully proofread your own writing for spelling, grammar and punctuation errors.

Some universities have bought into certain software packages – you should find out if this is the case and how they could support your proofreading.

Recognizing your strengths and weaknesses in spelling, punctuation and grammar

For your next piece of writing complete the tasks below:

☐ Section off areas to focus on by using a ruler or a piece of card.

☐ Read out loud carefully, following the punctuation and check for flow and errors.

☐ Read again, focusing on spelling. If you use a spellchecker, pay particular attention to the results, but do not rely solely on them.

☐ Read again, focusing on grammar and word choices to check that your sentences flow and make sense.

Test your knowledge by answering the following questions

1 What are the different types of apostrophes? Give examples.

....

....

....

2 What is the difference between a sentence and a paragraph?

....

....

....

3 What is the acronym for an effective paragraph and what do the letters stand for?

....

....

....

4 What is a homophone? Give three examples.

....

....

....

....

5 Give an example of the correct use of a colon.

....

....

....

....

6 Give an example of the correct use of a semicolon.

....

....

....

....

Based on the answers above, what areas do you feel you need to
explore further to develop your understanding?

....

....

....

....

....

....

....

How can I ensure my writing content is appropriate?

10 second summary

During the proofreading process, it is important to consider whether you have met the criteria that have been set for the intended assignment. Are you sure you have done what was asked?

What I *want* to write versus what I *need* to write

Many students have written perfectly good essays but have failed the
assignment because they misunderstood the instructions/essay question or have not paid enough attention to what they were asked to do.

You will be given some guidance material about what your essay should
include, and you should use this carefully to inform the content of your
essay. If based around a question, check that you have thoroughly
answered it. Could someone guess the question from your essay's
content? Is the main content relevant to the topic of discussion?

Carrying out a content check can help to ensure that you have met the
criteria set by your institution.

Relevance

You will need to use your own judgement when deciding what content to include in your essay. You will have read around the topic and a key skill in essay writing is selecting relevant material and content to include and disregarding irrelevant details. You must demonstrate that the overall focus is around the key essay question or topic and that this is up to date and relevant at the time of writing the essay.

Structure

Planning the structure is important in ensuring that you have met the assignment criteria. During the fine-tuning process, you should check that your structure is relevant and appropriate for the essay title or question.

Students will often plan their structure and then get carried away and go off on a tangent. It is always useful to have the essay title or question close to hand so you can constantly refer back to it and check that your content is still appropriate.

Instruction words

Look out for instruction words in your essay title or guidance materials such as:

Explain	Compare and contrast	Describe
Discuss	Examine	Assess
Analyse	Debate	Interpret
Evaluate	Investigate	Consider

Then make sure you know the specific meaning of these words, as they can give you a clue about the type of content you need to include. For example, if an essay title uses the word 'evaluate' it tells you that you need to consider both sides of an argument, or the pros and cons of the topic of the essay.

If you are asked to 'critically evaluate' a theoretical approach you will need to demonstrate an understanding of the approach, as well as other common approaches, and then weigh up the pros and cons of the theory and reach a confident and justified conclusion.

Top tip for using guidance

Highlight key instructions and key words in the guidance and use them as a checklist when proofreading the content of your writing.

For example, below is an example assignment brief and I have highlighted some words that seem important:

> For this assignment, write a 1,500 word philosophy statement about your views on education. This should represent your personal values and beliefs about effective teaching and learning. You need to consider how your philosophy has changed over time. You should use examples from your own experience at school. You should draw upon a range of literary sources to support your key points. Your writing should include coherent points and consider some opposing arguments.

These highlighted points can be used as a checklist when proofreading as in the example below:

> Have I …
>
> … given my views of education?
>
> … discussed my personal values and beliefs?
>
> … explored how my philosophy has changed?
>
> … provided my own examples?
>
> … used a range of literary sources?
>
> … ensured all my points are coherent?
>
> … included some opposing arguments?

'Make sure you don't write an essay about something you want to write about rather than what you have been asked to write about!'

Fine-tune your introduction

Your introduction allows you to set the scene and demonstrates to the marker that you understand the assignment brief, essay question or title and have given it careful consideration. You need to assure the reader that you haven't misinterpreted what you have been asked to do.

The introduction:

- Sets out the topic and engages the reader

- Introduces the context and background

- Outlines the key points or arguments to be discussed

If your introduction is poor and doesn't fit the expectations of the assignment brief or essay question it could lower the reader's expectations even before they read the whole essay.

A student told us

'I found that sometimes I could get carried away and start drifting onto another area as I found it interesting. Now I make sure I always have the essay title or question next to me, so I am constantly checking I am on track.'

Fine-tune your conclusion

Your conclusion gives you the opportunity to refer to the essay title or guidance to demonstrate that you have included relevant material and answered the question. Here are some things to look out for when checking your conclusion:

- Use words from the original title or question to demonstrate that you have covered them.

- Provide a brief recap of the main content of your essay to demonstrate that it is relevant.

- Draw attention to any significant points.

- Provide a brief evaluation of the key issues or arguments.

- Draw together the question, evidence and overall conclusion.

Look at some assignment guidance you have been given and follow the steps below. Do this both before starting your writing and again at the end, before proofreading your writing.

☐ Highlight key points from the guidance that give clues to a possible structure.

☐ Highlight key words that you feel are important to include in your writing.

☐ Create your own content checklist like the example provided on page 74.

☐ Check your completed essay against this checklist.

☐ Are your introduction and conclusion appropriate to the essay title, question or assignment brief?

How can I add criticality into my essay writing?

10 second summary

Criticality involves interpretation, analysis and evaluation. This should be something you look out for when carrying out the final checks of your essay as it is often where you can gain higher marks.

The word 'critical' can come across as being negative so it is easy to think that adding criticality means to simply find a fault or problem. However, this isn't the case. A critical essay is positive as it carefully interprets, explains, evaluates and analyses rather than being judgemental or disparaging.

Critical writing isn't just putting some quotes together and writing 'X says this, Y says this, and Z says this.' You need to look more deeply into the information and build on it to come up with your own argument and key points.

> 'Adding criticality to your essay writing does not mean you just criticize something.'

What are the key features of critical writing?

- Provides a very clear account rather than just accepting what has been said around a given topic.

- Any key points or arguments are always backed up with evidence.

- Provides a balanced approach to the strengths and weaknesses of different ideas.

- Justifies conclusions with clear evidence.

- Recognizes limitations of the evidence or argument.

- Doesn't rely on your own ideas. You need to use a range of sources to support what you are saying.

Be a detective!

- In order to include criticality in your writing, you will need to use evidence from other writers. You need to be like a detective finding multiple sources of information to build up a picture.

- This evidence will need analysing in terms of evaluating the different conclusions from a range of sources. These sources of evidence might be journal articles, scholarly publications, books, government documents, etc.

- You might also consider the strengths, weaknesses and reliability of this evidence. Is it recent? Is it from the country you are writing about? How credible is the author?

- Once you have explored, analysed and evaluated you should have a clear line of reasoning to lead to your conclusion.

A student told us

'If I were to provide any advice regarding criticality, I would champion the importance of it within academic work. It empowers you to bridge the gap between basic thinking and evaluative thinking – an aspect which will heighten your grades if done effectively.'

Critical or descriptive?

Students might get feedback such as 'Your writing is too descriptive' and this can be confusing because you might think that if you are describing something well, it is a good thing! However, in academic writing you shouldn't just be telling the reader about something, you need to be weighing up the evidence which will lead to your conclusion.

What is the difference between critical and descriptive writing?

Descriptive writing	Critical writing
Sets the background and provides evidence.	Develops an argument according to the evidence provided.
Takes something at face value.	Considers the quality and reliability of the evidence and argument.
Represents something as it stands.	Analyses and discusses around the topic in detail, reaching conclusions by weighing up the evidence.
Describes the qualities of something and identifies links between pieces of information.	Assesses the strengths and weaknesses. Indicates the relevance of links between different pieces of information.
States what a theory has said and informs the reader.	Argues the suitability and relevance of a theory and attempts to persuade the reader.
Lists things in order.	Considers the importance and relevance and structures the information accordingly.
Says how to do something.	Analyses *why* something is completed in a certain way.

What does this look like?

Here are examples of descriptive and critical writing.

Descriptive

Assertive discipline is a behavioural approach developed by Lee Canter in the 1970s and states that a teacher needs to have a clear set of boundaries and rules in the classroom which are shared with the children. Dreikurs (1968) thinks that the teacher should be the facilitator and that children can learn social skills through each other.

Critical

The assertive discipline approach is derived from a discipline system that relies on children following the rules set by the teacher (Canter, 1970). However, it could be suggested that this doesn't consider the different needs and personalities of children who might benefit from a more flexible discipline policy. This is supported by Dreikurs (1968) who instead believes that children should be involved in the discussions and rules that affect them and that this will motivate them to comply and reflect on their behaviour.

What is the PEEL structure?

A useful way to ensure you are adding criticality in your writing is to follow the PEEL structure when constructing your paragraphs.

P – Point (a clear opening topic sentence)

E – Evidence (to support the key point)

E – Explanation (how the evidence supports the key point)

L – Link (back to the main idea or bridge to the next paragraph)

Point

The environment practitioners create could be said to be instrumental in supporting the development of communication skills in children.

Evidence

Jarman (2008) believes that supportive environments influence development by encouraging discussion and problem solving. Supporting this, Biddle et al. (2013) found that poorly designed environments do not support development as they fail to provide opportunities for communicative play and can therefore encourage negative interactions.

Explanation

Although the article by Jarman (2008) was written about the impact on mathematical language, the overarching conclusion is that if the learning environment is set up effectively, it can facilitate communication by encouraging social interaction.

Link

This suggests that the environment children play within can have a significant impact on communication development and is therefore an important consideration for education practitioners.

CHECK POINT — Can you write your own critical paragraph?

Check your understanding of criticality by having a go at writing your own paragraph, following the PEEL structure, on a topic of your choice.

Point

....

....

....

....

....

....

....

Evidence

....

....

....

....

....

....

Explanation

Link

What should I look out for when proofreading for formatting issues?

10 second summary

Formatting errors can detract from the overall impression of your writing, so create a better impression by making sure that your writing is well presented.

Looking good!

Having inconsistencies in your font sizes, margins and headings can make your writing look disorganized and untidy. Well-formatted writing looks more professional and is more inviting for the reader.

You might be given guidelines from your institution about how to format your writing, so it is important that you pay close attention to these. This guidance might include, for example, having a title page or stipulating certain margin or font sizes. You might also be asked to use a specific font or line spacing.

Formatting also refers to the need to format quotations, citations and reference lists correctly.

Do I need a title page?

You might be asked to provide a title page with your essay. This is the very first page of your essay and includes all the important information such as the title of the essay, your name, your student number, the date and the word count.

Failing to include one when you have been asked to could create a negative impression on the reader.

What about page numbers?

Page numbers can help keep things in the right order and help the reader navigate the essay. Page numbers are relatively easy to add in documents and can be customized in terms of their font and location on the page.

Should margins be a certain size?

These might be specified, but as a rule you should use a minimum of 2.5 to a maximum of 3cm all the way round.

What about spacing?

Some universities will state that they require the essay to be double or 1.5 spaced. You should check this with your institution.

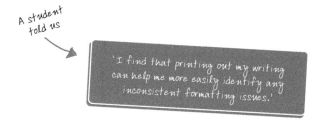

A student told us

'I find that printing out my writing can help me more easily identify any inconsistent formatting issues.'

Any particular font?

You should check with your institution if they require a particular font, but a popular choice for essays is Times New Roman because it is an easy font to read. The size of the font is usually 12 for text and 14 for headings. Make sure this is consistent throughout as it can look untidy if there is a sudden change of font style or size within an essay.

Should I use headings?

Headings are different to a title as they only refer to specific content in a section or chapter.

You should only use headings where they are stipulated. It would be a good idea to check with your tutor if you would like to use them in your essay and you can't find any guidance from your university.

What should headings do?

- Make the essay easier to navigate.

- Organize the content into different sections.

- They should be a consistent font and size throughout the essay.

- They should be clear and concise.

- The wording shouldn't be repetitive or similar to other headings.

Many computer software programs have heading features that enable you to automatically generate headings with the correct font and size. These can also be used to generate a table of contents which can be useful for longer essays or dissertations.

Align the alignment!

Again, you should check your university guidelines. You might think that justified text looks better, but your tutor might disagree!

The main thing is to make sure that the alignment is consistent throughout. There is nothing worse than reading an essay with lots of differently aligned text; this implies a lack of care and attention.

'A well formatted essay is much more inviting to read than an untidy one!'

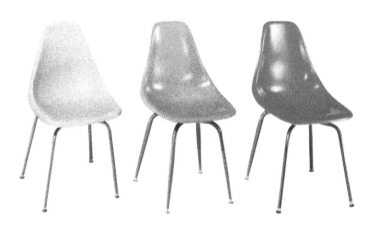

Does my writing need an appendix?

The appendix is found at the end of the essay and contains information that could be useful background or contextual information. You should check if an appendix is required for your essay.

The content is referred to and summarized in the main body of the essay and the reader is directed to where the information can be found (e.g. 'Appendix 1'). For example, the essay writer might be summarizing the results of an interview they carried out in their research and provide the full transcript of the interview in the appendix.

The formatting of citations

You need to check that your citations or quotations have followed the formatting guidelines provided by your institution. During the fine-tuning process, it is a good idea to check all your citations, including direct quotes and paraphrasing, to ensure they are presented correctly.

Is my referencing correct?

The purpose of referencing is to make clear where you obtained your information and to give the author credit. Accurate referencing will also help you avoid any accusations of plagiarism. The reader should always be able to easily find the source of your information with your accurate reference.

Remember that your institution might use a different referencing style from the literature you are reading. You should therefore be careful not to simply copy citations or references. You need to find out what the referencing style is for your university and follow this closely.

The following three references demonstrate different referencing styles for the same publication:

Harvard

Dolan, A.M. (2021). *Teaching climate change in primary schools: an interdisciplinary process*. Abingdon, Oxon; New York, NY: Routledge.

MLA 8

Dolan, Anne M. *Teaching Climate Change in Primary Schools: An Interdisciplinary Process*. Abingdon, Oxon; New York, NY, Routledge, 2021.

APA 7

Dolan, A. M. (2021). *Teaching climate change in primary schools: an interdisciplinary process*. Routledge.

Formatting check!

Use the checklist below to check the formatting of your essay.

Have I …?

☐ added a title page (if required)?

☐ added page numbers?

☐ used the appropriate margin size and is this consistent throughout?

☐ used the appropriate spacing and is this consistent throughout?

☐ used an appropriate font and is this consistent and the correct size throughout?

☐ used headings which are appropriate and correctly formatted?

☐ aligned my essay consistently throughout?

☐ checked that all my citations are in the correct format?

☐ checked that my reference list is accurate and in the correct format?

☐ checked that my appendices are complete and the cross-references in the essay correspond to the correct part of the appendices?

Congratulations

You now know that certain words and phrases should be avoided in your essay as well as finding out how to make your writing sound more professional. You should have some clear ideas about how to check for spelling, punctuation and grammar errors and the common mistakes to look out for. You also know about the importance of consistent and accurate formatting of your essays to make them look more inviting to the reader.

Where can I get help or support?

10 second
summary

You might need further support so it is important to know where you can get this support from. This section will give you some suggestions.

60 Second
summary

Help! Where can I find it?

You will probably have specific questions about your particular essay or assignment, and you should not be afraid to ask for further help or clarification if you need it. Your tutors at university want you to succeed and do well on your assignments so they will be willing to help.

Assistance might come in different forms, from support from your tutor to additional workshops or sessions. You might also be pointed in the direction of specific resources such as online material.

Support might not always come only from your university. Friends and family can also offer a supportive network and should be utilized!

Why do I need a supportive network of family and friends?

It is important to build and maintain a network of people you can turn to when needed. This doesn't mean you should try and get as many friends as you can! Instead, it is beneficial to have a handful of people around you who you can turn to in times of difficulty.

Periods when you are writing essays and needing to meet deadlines can be stressful at university, so it is important to have people around you to offer encouragement and advice. It can also be useful to speak to other students who are completing the same assignment as you, not to copy from each other but to give mutual encouragement.

You could also ask a friend or family member to proofread your essay as it can be useful to get feedback from someone who doesn't know much about your subject to check you are being clear or explicit. Someone who has good literacy skills could also help in terms of checking your spelling, punctuation or grammar.

A student told us

'Utilize others around you – having someone unfamiliar with your subject look at your work is always beneficial because it makes sure you are being precise and clear.'

Where else can I go for help?

'One of the biggest mistakes you can make at university is not asking for help.'

Personal tutor or member of staff

There might be external reasons for why you are struggling with your essay, such as issues at home or mental health difficulties. In this scenario you should speak to your personal tutor or a member of staff from your course. Even if they are unable to help directly, they are often the gateway to wider student support from the institution and can point you in the right direction. They will also know if you can ask for an extension or follow any other processes that would support you.

Some tutors are also able to look at a part or even all of your essay prior to submission and give you some general feedback. You should check with your individual institution if this is allowed and what specific support your tutor can offer in relation to your essay writing.

Academic support

Most universities have a department designed to support students with their academic studies. They often have a team of experts who can offer support to students with their academic writing and assignments. You might be able to book an appointment or access an appropriate workshop.

These departments usually have a bank of online resources that students can access to support them with specific areas such as 'Writing a literature review' or 'Writing critically'.

Workshops

Specific courses or schools within institutions often run their own workshops to support students within their department. These can be particularly useful as they are often planned around aspects of assignments that students have found challenging in the past. Or sometimes they are responsive to specific cohorts who might be struggling in a particular area.

IT support

If you are having difficulties with formatting your essay, for example if you wanted to know how to add a table of contents, institutions usually have an IT department where you can get support on using software tools or with other IT problems that might arise. You might spend ages trying to overcome an IT issue when simply asking for help will resolve it much more quickly – and develop your IT skills at the same time.

Student advice

Student advice or similar services can usually offer free, confidential and impartial advice. They can offer mental health support such as counselling or other advice such as about finances, benefit applications or accommodation. This can be useful if any of these issues are affecting your ability to complete your assignments.

Community support

Remember that your can also access support in your community, such as Citizens Advice, your GP, local mental health services or housing. There might also be local academic writing groups run externally that you could access.

Online support

There is a wealth of materials online that you can access. They can range from resources to help with aspects of academic writing, to online social media forums where you can communicate with other students.

Always bear in mind that online materials tend to be quite generic. You should always check with your institution for the specific details for your particular essay or assignment.

Where can I get help?

Use the questions below to identify the specific help you can access.

1 Who are members of your friends and family support network?

....

....

....

....

2 Who is your personal tutor and what support can they offer regarding your essay writing?

....

....

....

....

....

3 Where can you get support for academic writing from your institution?

....

....

....

....

....

4   Where can you get support for issues such as mental health and finances, etc. from your institution?

....

....

....

....

5   What support is there in your local community that might help with your assignments?

....

....

....

....

6   Does your department recommend any specific online materials to support your assignments?

....

....

....

....

7   Are you a member of an online support network?

....

....

....

....

Congratulations

Well done! You now know how to proofread and improve your essay!

Final checklist: How to know you are done

Now you should be in a much better position to proofread your essay and hopefully achieve higher marks!

Use this final checklist as a reminder:

Preparing to proofread

1 Have you identified a quiet and calm space as well as a
  specific time to complete your proofreading?   Yes/No

2 Have you removed any distractions around you – noise,
  phone, TV, etc.?   Yes/No

Proofreading for clarity

3 Are your key points clear and concise as well as having an
  appropriate tone for the intended audience?   Yes/No

4 Does your writing flow well and is it easy to read?   Yes/No

5 Do your paragraphs look the correct length and contain
   appropriate content and structure?   Yes/No

Proofreading for spelling, grammar and punctuation.

6 Have you read your writing out loud several times and
  followed the punctuation carefully to check for errors?   Yes/No

Proofreading for appropriate content and criticality

7 Have you highlighted the key words or phrases in your
  assignment guidance and completed your own proofreading
  checklist and used this to check your writing?   Yes/No

8 Is the structure logical and does it provide clear stepping
  stones for the reader?   Yes/No

Proofreading for formatting

9 Is your writing in the correct font and text size recommended
  by your institution and is this consistent throughout?   Yes/No

10 Are page numbers, headers and footers, citations and
   margin sizes correct?   Yes/No

How do I know when I have finished proofreading?

Once you have proofread your writing several times and have answered
yes to all the checklist points, you should be finished! However, remember it is always good to get a fresh pair of eyes on your writing so try to
ask someone else to read it through too!

Glossary

Appropriate content   Correct or suitable information.

Appendix   A section of an essay containing supplementary information.

Citation   A reference to a book, paper or author.

Clarity   Clear expression.

Consistency   A feature, such as alignment, is the same throughout the assignment.

Distraction   Something that directs or diverts attention away.

Environment   Surroundings or conditions a person operates in.

Essay conclusion   The final section of an essay.

Essay introduction   The opening section of an essay.

Formatting   Arranging the appearance or presentation.

Instruction words   Words that tell an individual what to do.

Proofreading   Carefully checking for errors in text.

References   Detailed information on the sources used.

Repetitive writing   Using the same word, phrase or key point over and over again.

Supportive network   People who support an individual in achieving their goals.

Title page   A page at or near the front of an essay that displays key information.

Further resources

Books

Baratta, A. (2020). *Read critically*. Super quick skills. Sage Publications.

Chatfield, T. (2019). *Think critically*. Super quick skills book. Sage Publications.

Coleman, H. (2019). *Polish your academic writing*. Super quick skills. Sage Publications.

Websites

Cite this for me. Reference-generating software that creates in-text references and reference lists/bibliographies: https://citethisforme.com

Google Scholar. An academic search engine to access academic papers, journals and other scholarly sources. Free of charge although not all resources are free: https://scholar.google.com

Grammarly. An online app that checks grammar and vocabulary. The basic checker is free, but it has many premium features for an additional cost: https://www.grammarly.com

Manchester Phrasebank. A general resource for academic writers to provide ideas of words and phrases to communicate clearly in academic writing: https://www.phrasebank.manchester.ac.uk

Milton Keynes UK
Ingram Content Group UK Ltd.
UKHW021458021224
3319UKWH00038B/824